Blood Moon

Elaine S. Nussbaum

A Publication of The Poetry Box®

Poems ©2022 Elaine S. Nussbaum
All rights reserved.

Editing & Book Design by Shawn Aveningo Sanders
Cover Design by Shawn Aveningo Sanders
 (using photos provided by Elaine S. Nussbaum)
Author Photo by David Scharf

No part of this book may be reproduced in any manner whatsoever without permission from the author, except in the case of brief quotations embodied in critical essays, reviews and articles.

ISBN: 978-1-956285-14-7
Printed in the United States of America.
Wholesale distribution via Ingram.

Published by The Poetry Box®, August 2022
Portland, Oregon
https://ThePoetryBox.com

*Be calm. Do not give in
to the rabid red throat of age. In a red world, imprint
the valentine and blush of romance for the dark.
It has come. You will not be this quick-to-redden
forever. You will be green again, again and again.*

—Marvin Bell, *Mars Being Red*
(Copper Canyon Press, 2004)

Contents

The Color of Blood	7
Blue Jay	8
What Do I Do about *The New York Times*?	9
This Holy Week	11
Cattails	14
Touch	15
Ultraviolet Light	16
May Day During Covid-19	17
Middle of May	18
Moonshine	19
Ode to Moka Pot	20
Ash	22
Google Tells Me What I Thought Were Cabbage Moths Are Really Butterflies	23
A Crow Is a Corvid	24
Mushrooms	25
Blood Moon	26
Premonition	28
Hummingbird	29
I Dream I Grow My Hair Long	30
Pendulum	32
Joseph Canyon	34
When the Rooster Stops Crowing	35
Despair	36
Raven	37
Acknowledgments	39
Early Praise for *Blood Moon*	41
About the Author	43

The Color of Blood
March 7, 2020

Bloody Sunday. US Representative John Lewis urges voters to use the ballot box as *a nonviolent instrument to redeem the soul of America*. In 1965, civil rights marchers are gassed and beaten with billy-clubs as they cross Edmund Pettus Bridge. John Lewis is bashed in the skull.

Women in scarlet gowns spread out over downtown Portland warning of catastrophic climate change caused by human activity. Bloody handprints on faces symbolize the missing and murdered indigenous women and men. Almost 10,000 missing and murdered in the US and Canada.

Pandemic. Alternate facts. We are all living in a Sci-fi apocalyptic movie. On TV a Coronavirus model is shown over and over—a gray lipid envelope studded with scarlet rosettes the color of blood. In my spare bedroom three baby chicks chirp from their temporary home. This dark world is waking up. My rooster crows. His call is answered by another, then another, then another.

Blue Jay

Plum blossoms fall like snow. A Steller's
jay, with its charcoal-colored topknot
and sapphire tail feathers, collects dead
grass to build a nest in the alder tree,
where he and his mate will squawk and
squawk. I don't know until I turn on my TV
that in New York City, 1,900 people died
in the last 72 hours, doubling the number
in the previous 72. Outside hospitals, bodies
are loaded into refrigerated morgue trucks
by gurney and forklift. The first infant has died,
and one-million people world-wide have contracted
Covid-19, doubling the number in one week.

What Do I Do about *The New York Times?*

...that nests securely in the box along with the local paper? Coronavirus lasts 24 hours on paper, but several days on plastic. Frost blankets the half-planted vegetable beds. The rooster crows, and three baby chicks chirp from their home in a plastic tub. Wearing my red fingerless gloves, I collect the papers from the box and place them on the back porch. After gingerly removing the plastic wrappers, I stuff the plastic into the recycle and flatten the papers onto the dryer. I wait until the next day to read *The New York Times*.

To make it last longer, I place two scoops of the good coffee and two scoops of not-so-good coffee into the grinder. The soy creamer I like is almost gone. I turn the carton over and prop it up in the refrigerator, so I get every goddamn drop. I have only six chocolate chip cookies left. I am quarantined for ten more days. If I have one-half a cookie per night, I will make it.

The only vehicles on the road are log trucks carrying pecker poles. The trucks go by two or three times per day, jake brakes squealing. A small plane breaks the silence. No jets fly overhead. A lawn mower whines, the creek babbles. I hear children laughing. A young mother and two kids pick up trash along the road and place it in a plastic garbage sack. My friend Meg calls and asks if I need anything from the feed store. *Yes, a bag of rice hulls and some oyster shells.* This is the way we used to live. This is the way we are supposed to live.

Because of Covid-19, only 2 of any item allowed for purchase. The length of two shopping carts end-to-end is 6 feet the sign on the door of Grocery Outlet reads. A manager tells a customer *We are keeping the restrooms locked now. Is that to prevent people from stealing toilet paper?* the customer asks. *Of course, it is* I say out loud to a wall of toothpaste and mouthwash. Then to myself, *Has it come to this?* As I walk towards the bread aisle, I encounter two elderly ladies. I stop six feet shy of them. They ask, *Are we okay? Yes, we are all okay,* I reply and let them pass.

[. . .]

Even though Governor Brown strongly urged everyone to stay home this weekend, throngs of tourists stormed onto the Oregon beaches and into the tiny towns along the coast. While I am painstakingly spraying a beach solution on each package of frozen spinach from the grocery, others are laughing and spraying infected droplets at gas stations on the way to the coast or the mountains or the desert.

> This is a nightmare
> we will wake up from.
> The rufus hummingbird
> still searches for sugar water
> in the red-based feeder.

This Holy Week

*The U.S. Surgeon General declares this week
will be the 'hardest and saddest' for most Americans*

Tuesday's super moon will appear like emerald-pink phlox.
In Florida, another gender reveal party explodes into flame.
Coronavirus appears as a lipid envelope studded with rosettes
clustered in triangles, mingling with orange and gray proteins.

In Florida, another gender reveal party explodes into flame,
and coronavirus cases explode to over one hundred thousand.
Clustered in triangles, mingling with orange and gray proteins.
Palm Sunday and the churches in Florida are packed to the brim.

Coronavirus cases explode to over one hundred thousand
in Florida. In the USA, one person is dying every 45 seconds.
Palm Sunday and the churches in Florida are packed to the brim.
They are laughing and dancing, rejoicing and singing the hymns

in Florida. In the USA, one person is dying every 45 seconds.
In reality, the moon looks like a white money plant, *Lunarai annua*.
They are laughing and dancing, rejoicing and singing the hymns.
In Dutch speaking countries, *judaspenning* means "coins of Judas."

In reality, the moon looks like a white money plant, *Lunarai annua*.
A NYC paramedic: "Out here on the streets, it's nothing but sirens."
In Dutch speaking countries, *judaspenning* means "coins of Judas."
In New York, there are not enough cemeteries to bury the dead.

A NYC paramedic: "Out here on the streets, it's nothing but sirens."
He responded to sixteen cardiac arrest calls in twelve hours.
In New York, there are not enough cemeteries to bury the dead.
Passover tonight. *Why is this night different from all other nights?*

[. . .]

He responded to sixteen cardiac arrest calls in twelve hours.
From my writing cabin in Oregon, I see the cedar's lacy branches.
Passover tonight. *Why is this night different from all other nights?*
I see the sunlight skimming the moss-covered trunks of alder.

From my writing cabin in Oregon, I see the cedar's lacy branches.
A murder of crows erupts into cacophony, settles into the fir trees.
I see the sunlight skimming the moss-covered trunks of alder.
The crow's cacophony ignites the tree frogs into peals of croaking.

A murder of crows erupts into cacophony, settles into the fir trees.
… by Easter Sunday; we'll have packed churches all over this country.
The crow's cacophony ignites the tree frogs into peals of croaking.
Holy Thursday. Christ predicts his betrayal, his death, his resurrection.

… by Easter Sunday; we'll have packed churches all over this country.
As I am writing, I hear a loud crash. I discover a fallen tree.
Holy Thursday. Christ predicts his betrayal, his death, his resurrection.
In New York, 779 people died in 24 hours, the highest in one day.

As I am writing, I hear a loud crash. I discover a tree has fallen.
Governor Cuomo, who is not Jewish, reminds us it is Passover.
In New York, 779 people died in 24 hours, the highest in one day.
We learn from the past. Next year we will reach the Promised Land.

Governor Cuomo, who is not Jewish, reminds us it is Passover.
Cuomo tells us there is good news; the curve is flattening.
We learn from the past. Next year we will reach the Promised Land.
In NYC, new hospitalizations in one day decreased 69 percent.

Cuomo tells us there is good news; the curve is flattening.
Black Saturday. The day between the crucifixion and resurrection.
In NYC, new hospitalizations in one day decreased 69 percent.
As observant Jews, they could not bury Jesus until Sunday.

Black Saturday. The day between the crucifixion and resurrection.
In New York, a third-grade teacher dies of coronavirus.
As observant Jews, they could not bury Jesus until Sunday.
St. Patrick's was converted to a field hospital. Now, they don't need it.

In New York, a third-grade teacher dies of coronavirus.
Walking to my writing cabin, I scare up two yearling blacktail deer.
St. Patrick's was converted to a field hospital. Now, they don't need it.
The deer nibble weeds in the sunshine; their black tails flick as I write.

Tuesday's super moon did not appear like emerald pink phlox.
Coronavirus appears as a lipid envelope studded with rosettes.

Cattails

As I enter the local supermarket, Tracy Chapman's "Talkin' Bout a Revolution" blares from the speakers and swallows chatter from their home in the rafters. 8:00 a.m. Do you wear a blue surgical mask, an N95 carpenter's dust-mask, a fern-patterned cotton mask, or a black neoprene mask you paid way too much for, that squeezes your nose so tight it leaves a red mark, but not nearly as bad as the marks you see broadcast on the faces of the front-line medical workers after a 12-hour shift? Are you the older couple without masks, who stand in front of the only plastic bag dispenser in the produce aisle and discuss your next purchase, while four or five other people wait six feet away, radiating out from you like a human sunflower? On your drive home, the sun streaks through your windshield. Perched on cattails, Red-winged blackbirds serenade you from the glittering marsh.

Touch

At the hardware store I pick up a cucumber plant and a bag of potting soil. When I hand the cashier the plant, my pinky finger grazes the back of her hand. This is the first time I have touched another human, except my husband, in eleven weeks.

Ultraviolet Light

Lilac blossoms begin as purple pearls,
and wisteria as fuzzy caterpillar-like
blossoms. It's not because my spring
allergies are worse when it rains, it's
because I put the store-bought green
onions on the black tile countertop
before they had been washed that
I developed this dry cough. Trump asks
the medical experts, as far as disinfectant...
*is there a way we can do something like
that by injection inside or almost a cleaning...*
The next day the Maryland Health Department
receives 100 calls asking if it is safe to ingest
disinfectant. Lysol issues a statement warning
against any internal use of their products.
Fuchsia-colored blooms explode today.
Could we hit the body with ultraviolet light?

May Day During Covid-19

My husband comes to me in a dream.
He has been dead thirty years, struck
by a car in Ecuador. Because his body
was so far gone by the time it arrived
in the States, the undertaker would
not let me see him. I often dream he
fabricated his own is death, that he
is alive and living the dream in Ecuador.
But in this dream, he tells me, *This Covid-19
pandemic—you will all be okay.* I often
dream my mother is still alive, that she
was buried alive, and after many years,
escapes. I think about the thousands
of humans who will not get to say
goodbye to their loved ones.

The Camellia bush behind my compost,
that has not bloomed in sixteen years,
produces two exquisite pink blossoms.

Middle of May

The garden bed is filled with cat shit, slugs and weeds.
The government is filled with liars, fakes and spies.

There's shit in the bowl, the toilet is plugged.
How many days since you've been hugged?
There's hair in my mouth, and mice in the tub.

Moonshine

At night the full moon shears through clouds lighting up the yard with a milky glow. Strawberry Moon. Only three weeks since George Floyd was lynched by four Minneapolis police officers. Social distancing flies out the window when my neighbor brings over his corn liquor hooch, and after dinner outside, where we all sit six feet apart and eat baby back-ribs marinated in molasses and brown sugar, my neighbor pours one too many shots. When he stands to leave, he topples over on top of me.

Ode to Moka Pot

I love its shape—an hourglass, a vessel, the shape of a woman.
Its plastic handle broke off years ago. To begin, I fill the bottom
chamber with water, but only up to the release valve. Too full,
it could explode, and pieces of metal and plastic could fly
all over the room. Coffee could end up on the ceiling. People
could be injured. I fill the middle chamber with exactly two scoops
of Peet's Organic Alma de la Tierra dark roast. Soul of the Earth.
Brewing on a gas stove, my Moka pot produces only 1 to 2 bars
of pressure, while true espresso needs 8 to 10 bars. The Moka pot
was invented by Alfonso Bialetti, in 1930, during Mussolini's fascist
regime. He was inspired to make the Moka pot while watching his wife
do laundry.

This nation has become a pressure cooker,
a Moka Pot, 15 bars. George Floyd gasps
I CAN'T BREATHE
as a blue knee is pressed to his neck for
8 minutes and 46 seconds
while three other officers assist,
and 17-year-old Darnella Frazier records
it on her phone. Rage explodes—in Minneapolis
and around the world. Anarchy, mobs, looting.
Hundreds of thousands under curfew orders.
When does rage turn to violence, to boiling point? NO.
NO. NO. Monster without a head, random
acts of violence, passion. Riot or peaceful protest?
A young black man worms his way into
the frame throwing out epithets, giving the finger
to America.

Signs read
WHITE SILENCE IS VIOLENCE.
and AN EYE FOR AN EYE
LEAVES EVERYONE BLIND. America is burning.
Rage turns to outrage.
VANDALIZE THE SITUATION. BLACK
LIVES MATTER. WHAT SIDE ARE YOU ON?
STALEMATE! THEY DON'T WANT
TO REOPEN THE COUNTRY, THEY JUST WANT
BLACK FOLKS TO GO BACK TO WORK.
But *maga loves African-Americans
maga loves black people.*

The president pronounces martial law, invokes the 1807 Insurrection Law for a photo op. He holds a bible upside down in front of St. John's Episcopal church. Tear gas swirls red and burning. Peaceful protesters. Pastor Gini Gerbasi falls to the floor because she doesn't know what is happening. Boogaloo Bois dressed in Hawaiian shirts with Pepe the Frog logos, carry AK47s. Boogaloo Bois, they want a Race War. Nazis, White Supremacists, Patriot Prayer and Proud Boys. Flash bangs and rubber bullets, seared into our collective memory. Seared into our hearts, the blue knee on the throat of George Floyd. George Floyd gasping for breath, calling for his mother
I can't breathe.

And the chant starts and goes around the world
I CAN'T BREATHE.
I CAN'T BREATHE.
I CAN'T
BREATHE.

Ash

While we pick grapes in the backyard, the sky turns a milky white.
Blasts of hot air and wind stir the green leaves to a frenzy—
a strong smell of smoke. Our neighbor thinks it's blowing up from
fires in Southern Oregon. Thirty major fires burn in California,
but the wind is blowing from the east.

A human-caused fire near Estacada begins in dry grass, and soon
spreads to timber and rough terrain. In Detroit—fifty miles as the crow
flies—south of Estacada, fire envelopes the town. A volunteer firefighter
films as he drives his family through the dense smoke. Fire licks at the edges
of the frame. *Is this normal? his son asks. No, son. It is anything but normal.*

A volunteer firefighter returns to Detroit to find black skeletons
of trees rising out of piles of white ash. Smoke, there is so much smoke.
Hunks of metal that used to be cars litter the landscape. The man is almost
weeping, *We had so much joy here, so much joy. I am sorry, I am so sorry.*
He seems to be talking to the town, the lake, the trees.

Google Tells Me What I Thought Were Cabbage Moths Are Really Butterflies

The Air Quality Index is 318, down from 453, but anything over 300 is *Hazardous*. Muggy. A few bees whiz around the snowberry bush and *Small White Butterflies* flit around the yellow broccoli flowers—broccoli gone to seed. I should have exterminated them, but they are so pretty—ivory-colored with two charcoal dots on each wing. They will lay their eggs on the cabbage leaves and tiny green caterpillars will emerge to eat their own shells before they begin to munch on the cabbage.

A Crow Is a Corvid

Jackson Hole, Wyoming

In the middle of the square, the one with the four arches made of 1,000 elk antlers, a raven caws. In the shade of a Ponderosa, as far away from anyone as I can get, I watch tourists from all over the world, lick ice cream and snap pictures with their phones. Only I wear a mask. The raven, perched on an aspen, its leaves ready to burst into flame, caws again, *People, winter is coming. Get your act together!*

Portland, Oregon

A siren screams, a crow caws. In a building across the street a child screams bloody murder. Bloody murder, what does that even mean? From my perch on a bench graffitied with roses I see a scattering of people who meander through this park. A teenage girl stretches her legs out at a picnic table, disappears into her phone. 3:30 in the afternoon and 81 degrees. It is a typical October afternoon, except it isn't. School should have started a month ago. Because of Covid, everything is shut except the mega-grocery across the street. Is the child hurt? Doesn't she want to get back on Zoom? The leaves are turning burgundy but have not begun to drop. A dog barks. The crow stares at me.

Mushrooms

Tents pop up like mushrooms in newly mowed grass—
brown, white, green, orange, and blue tents. Some people
don't have tents, only sleeping bags, some sleep in clothes
with more clothes piled on top. People in suits cross streets.
These people are sleep walking. Some tent encampments
are neat, some are littered with cardboard, needles, beer cans,
glass bottles, and blue plastic. A pink Flamingo, an iron horseshoe,
an artificial bougainvillea, an angel carved into a tree. An entire
household is stuffed into a shopping cart: bedroll, duffel bag, white
plastic tub filled with dirty dishes. Affixed to the side of the cart
is a sign: *coins or green stuff, deposit here.* From one tent, a kid
emerges, tucks in a white shirt so ripped, it's really only half a shirt,
shakes his black dreads. Down the block a red-headed kid punches
the air, punches the air with a gloved hand, punches over and over
as he walks down the sidewalk mumbling to the gray mushy air.
Once a day now, I am filled with rage, and want to punch the air
over and over until I can breathe again. In Oregon, 628 people died
today from Covid-19. We are all so tired. In the bike lane, a kid
rides a motorized scooter, ear buds blaring. Is his tune happy or dire?

Blood Moon
~for Marvin Bell

1. The Dead Woman and the Moon

The dead woman did not get much sleep because all night the
    cats jumped on her head.
This election is too close to call, and this moon is a Hunter's
    Blue.
Once in a blue moon the waxing gibbous moon sweeps past
    the red planet Mars.
Halloween and Civil War; the president will sulk in his bunker
    till the fatigues yank him out.
The dead woman cares not a whit for him, and this country is
    shriveling before our eyes.
Red, white, and blue, and the stars and stripes are whipping
    behind thousands of black trucks gunning and gunning and
    blowing black exhaust.
The flags are tattered at the edges and those monster trucks
    can't help dragging the flags through the mud.

2. More about the Dead Woman and the Moon

This blue moon is also a blood moon, and the dead woman has
 been sleep-walking.
If the dead woman is truly to write a dead woman poem, she
 must have kaleidoscopic perception, but the dead woman
 cannot wrap her head around the statistics.
The not-president is going for herd immunity, doesn't care if
 we all die.
All the dead people can't live without you Marvin, and the live
 people cannot die.
We are a country washed up on a beach after a shipwreck.
The tide is coming in, and the waves are getting closer.
It is raining and we are naked; We must make a fire, but all the
 wood is soaking wet.
Help will be coming in eighty days, but how do we get through
 this without eating each other?

Premonition
February 2020

Bravo Pod is the only detention classroom with a window. You look out on gray and razor wire. I am not supposed to turn off the lights, but I do. The boys have their feet up on their desks. Their sweatshirt hoods are pulled over their shaggy hair. We are watching CNN-10, the daily news show for students. Wuhan, China—A novel corona virus has been kept under wraps by Chinese officials. A short pimply-faced boy shouts *There will be a pandemic, and everyone will die.* Now—at the end of October—over one million people have died worldwide.

Hummingbird

The frequency of my cat's purr
        is the same frequency as the beating
                wings above our heads.

*

He just sits there turning his head from side to side
        sits on that slender wisteria branch, sits on that twisted
                and slender wisteria branch

turning his ruby-colored head, turning his glistening
        ruby-colored head in the gray and dripping evening,
                sits there, mere inches from the red-based feeder

or maybe he is standing. He stands there on feet
        the size of a pencil eraser stands there on the wet and twisted
                wisteria branch, while the cat underneath munches food.

*

The red-based feeder is empty. Ants crawl up and down
        inside the glass, sucking up the last of the nectar. The female
                hummingbird waits, waits totally still. She stands still

for a quarter of an hour, half an hour, three-quarters of an hour, while I
        eat my lunch. She turns her head a quarter turn, lifts her doll sized
                wings, scratches her side with a needle like beak.

*

Three hummingbirds buzz, spin fight over a teaspoon
        of sugar water left in the feeder. One screeches two feet
                from my head, *Why is there no food in the feeder?*

I Dream I Grow My Hair Long

1.

I dream I grow my hair long. Over and over, I dream this. I grow it and cut it, grow it long like it was when I was nineteen. I cut it before my teenage crush gets to see my long hair. He turns into my husband,

David. In real life I have not cut my hair since mid-February. It is now the end of May. 100,000 people in the US have died from Covid-19. My hair is to my shoulders and streaked with gray. David thinks if I keep

growing it, I will look like Bonnie Raitt. If only I could sing and play the blues like she can. We are at Phase 1. I could call my hairdresser whose husband is deployed somewhere in the Middle East, or maybe

they sent him home. Even though my hair falls in my eyes, and gets in my mouth when I eat, I don't make an appointment. I don't cut my hair.

2.

It has been a year and a week since I cut my hair. Now, 500,000 people have died. I dream of Michael Tinker. I can feel his blue and purple flannel shirt. The hair on his dark arms, below where he has rolled up his sleeves.

It is cold in his converted mail truck. He has a lot of stuff in there: tools, clothes, papers. His gorgeous dreads reach to the middle of his back. We smoke joint after joint to keep warm. Maybe sip whiskey. I am not

in love. I am nineteen; I don't know anything about sex. I have had sex with many men, but I really don't know anything. We drag a wooden kitchen chair outside and drape a white towel over my shoulders.

I lean against his long blue-jeaned legs. I feel the sun on my neck, and his fingers combing through my hair. Then he cuts it.

3.

I have celebrated two birthdays since the beginning of the Covid-19 outbreak. The president declares *this is not a game*. Now my hair is down to the middle of my back. The ends are dry and break off.

I call my hairdresser and get the same message: due to the Covid-19 pandemic, for the safety of our stylists... please be patient. I was not in love with Tinker because I was still in love with Duane. Sometimes

we made love in my house on the hill, Duane's dark hair sprinkled with plaster dust. He tasted like beer. My breasts are sweet and white under my paisley halter top. At the tavern we drink beer after beer

white foam sticking to our sweaty lips. No matter how long my hair gets, I will never be nineteen again. One out of 500 have died of Covid-19.

Pendulum

It's been a year since the World Health Organization declared Covid-19 a pandemic. International Women's Day. A year since David and I went to the Women's March wearing construction dust masks, and everyone looked at us like we were crazy. Now, I carry a mask everywhere, even up to my writing cabin, where I am more likely to meet a squirrel or doe than a human.

The canopy outside my studio is in ruins, flattened by two feet of snow that fell weeks ago. Now, the snow has melted, but the meadow looks like a war zone. Biden is president, but the hate and conspiracy still swirl around us. Some want a civil war. Things will never get back to normal, but were they ever normal? Half a million dead. A thousand still dying every day. A deadly coup. An epidemic of hatred and conspiracy. A storm brews outside my window. The limbs of the grandmother cedar sway, then shake. Creak. Branches fly in the wind and hit the roof.

Time has become compressed. This year has disappeared, and I am a year closer to death. I remember how scared we were a year ago. Would we all die of this thing? Memories come flooding back and I don't know if they are from yesterday, a year ago, ten years ago, or even my memories. One minute everything is possible, the next minute, nothing is possible. Is it fall or spring? It must be spring because the wild currant is beginning to bloom. Blursday. I walk into a room and forget what I came for. Is it early onset dementia? We are all so tired.

In a March 18 *Salon* essay, Nicole Karlis calls what I am feeling Pandemic Trauma and Stress Experience (PTSE). A psychotherapist in Chicago, tells *Salon* "…it could have to do with the fact that as a society, we've been living under the grip of chronic stress for one year now." The novelist and essayist Leslie James describes this year as a story without a clear narrative arc, which can be quite disturbing.

I think of it this way. Exactly two years ago, I attended a conference at the Portland Convention Center, along with thousands of other people. At the end of the convention, I sat under the Foucault pendulum located in an atrium between conference rooms. I recorded on my phone. Thousands of people were murmuring. A 900-pound brass globe swings on a 70-foot cable powered by electro magnetics. It swings 24 hours a day, 365 days a year. At the height of each swing, the globe pauses for a millisecond before swinging the other way.

This is where we are: in that millisecond before the pendulum swings the other way. Between the Covid-19 pandemic and no Covid-19. Between winter and spring. Between hate and love. Between truth and lies. Between myth and reality. Between life and death. We wait for the pendulum to swing the other way.

Joseph Canyon

1.

All night, the bitter taste of ash on my tongue. This morning the sun—an orange eye, an orb. Something is not right. Is this Mordor, this valley filled with smoke? Ash like dead ants drifts down onto this porch. I smell something dead. Rattlesnakes wither from every orifice on this parched land. Elderberry blossoms wither on the vine. This wind—Chief Joseph moaning.

2.

Hummingbirds gather at the red feeder—the only color for miles. The smoke clears, then rolls in again. Buzzards fly in slow sweeping circles. I have no idea what time it is. Smoke and the smell of sage. When the smoke clears: spruce, Fleabane, Quaking aspen, teasel weed, Ponderosa pine. Burned out hulk of a planet. These pines can withstand a lot, but we cannot.

3.

Fire evacuation switches from one to two. The fire is close, but I can't see flames. Wind from the northwest. All this smoke. The ghost of Chief Joseph is not happy. The ghost of the Nimipuu KNOW something is not right. Gnarled skeletons of burned trees rise black from last year's fire. All the predictions and we still do nothing.

When the Rooster Stops Crowing

We are going backwards in time, not forward in progress
—Dr. Kavita Patel

The rooster has stopped crowing and has trouble walking.
Grape-sized tumors bloom on his pink belly, where feathers
have fallen out. The hens' feathers are falling out also, leaving
pink flesh exposed on their backs above their tail feathers.

The Delta Corona virus appears to spread as easily as chicken
pox and causes more severe illness. There are as many new
cases now, as there were in early February. I walk into my local
grocery, slip the ear loops of my mask over my ears.

An elderly man finishes buttoning his blue jeans, so loose
they fall off his slender frame—plaid work shirt, cowboy boots.
A few paces behind, his wife tries to keep up. He glares at my
masked face. *We don't have to wear those anymore, you know!*

Did you get vaccinated? I ask. *Hell no! I am old. I don't care
if I die.* After dying during the heat wave, one blossom of my mother-in-
law's rose blooms scarlet, the same scarlet as my neighbor's carnations.
The rooster's feathers gleam florescent green in the noon day sun.

The hens' feathers are growing back too. Indigo pins with puffs
at the tips, push through pink skin. The rooster emits a feeble crow,
then a crow like a cow mooing, a crow like an old man clearing
his throat. His call is answered by another, then another, then another.

Despair

Everything is plundered, betrayed, sold,
Death's great black wing scrapes the air
Misery gnaws to the bone.
Why then do we not despair?
           —Anna Akhmatova

    Despair
        Hummingbird
    Despair
        Hummingbird
    Despair
        Hummingbird

    Pandemic brain
        AGAIN
    Insurrection
        AGAIN
    Heat dome
        AGAIN
    Afghanistan
        AGAIN
    Forest fires
        AGAIN

    No smoke   yet.

Raven

Third heat wave of the summer. 102 degrees.
I can tell they are ravens, by their deep sonorous
caws and series of clicks and knocks. A flap of wing.
Something swoops across my field of vision, disappears.

I dream great wings sweep, turn everything dark.
The ravens roost in the trees above our house: fir, cedar,
clumps of maple. I place some plums, grapes, dried bread-
crumbs in an egg carton, balance it on the roof.

I have heard that ravens bring gifts to those who feed them.
According to the Haida, Raven—though a trickster known for
gluttony, greed, and impatience—stole light and brought it into
this world, cracking it into shards: the sun, the moon, the stars.

Acknowledgments

Many thanks to the editors of these publications where the following poems were first published, sometimes in a different format:

Artists and Climate Change/100 Word Stories: "Blue Jay"

Persimmon Tree: "What Do I Do About the New York Times"

Headline Poetry and Press: "Ultraviolet Light"

Passager Journal/Pandemic Diaries: portions of "Ash"

Early Praise for *Blood Moon*

In this series of mostly prose poems, the reader's brought face to face with the immense malaise of our moment. The focus moves from the natural world to the various disasters surrounding us: homelessness, wildfires, Covid, social unrest. I admire the ordinary details of a life woven into the fabric of a poetry of witness. Check it out!

—Joseph Millar, author of *Dark Harvest*

Elaine Nussbaum's *Blood Moon* reads like a personal journal of the COVID pandemic with seemingly stream of consciousness observations, until you realize that by weaving past and present, national, and local events, she shows how each reflects on another. Sometimes the speed of happenings is dizzying as her images race through history along with the progress of the pandemic from early fears and errors to the exhaustion of two years later. She captures the sense of suspension we all felt, even as we went about daily life. Her view is both sweeping and micro-focused. World death count, presidential election, Western forest fires, the local grocery store, and birds outside her window. Are all connected?

—Sherry Rind, author of *Between States of Matter* and *The Store-House of Wonder and Astonishment*

The poems in *Blood Moon* are shards of light wrested from a dark and chaotic time in our history. Nussbaum journeys deep into our collective experience of the pandemic and emerges with poems of remarkable beauty and resonance. As the Covid death toll climbs, wildfires rage, and protestors clash in the streets, the poet struggles to make sense of the madness and draws strength and solace from the natural world: the changing seasons, cycles of the moon, and resiliency of wild creatures.

Nussbaum is a master of closely observed, finely rendered images: the feeling of a pinky finger grazing the back of a stranger's hand; ivory-colored butterflies *with two charcoal dots on each wing*.

[. . .]

Though firmly rooted in a specific moment time, these poems are about more than living through the pandemic. They are about how to keep our hearts open and our spirits intact even when the world is burning down around us. *This is a nightmare/ we will wake up from,* she writes. *The Rufus Hummingbird/ still searches for sugar water/ in the red-based feeder.*

—Gwen McNeir, author of *An Animal with Wings*

About the Author

Elaine Nussbaum lives in Scappoose, Oregon with her partner, David, three cats, five hens and a rooster named Echinacea. When she is not working as a substitute teacher at a juvenile detention facility, infusing poetry into the curriculum, she is writing in her cabin surrounded by 3 and 1/2 acres of second growth forest. Every fall, salmon spawn in the creek which runs through her front yard. In her spare time, Ms. Nussbaum enjoys cross-country skiing and sea kayaking. Currently, she and David are restoring a 37-foot sailboat, and plan to sail the inside passage to Alaska next summer.

Ms. Nussbaum holds an MFA in Writing from Pacific University (2013), and a Certificate in Writing from the Jack Kerouac School of Disembodied Poetics at Boulder University (1986). Her work has appeared in *Poetry Seattle, Bombay Gin, The Sun, Spilt Infinitive, Louisiana Literature, Silk Road, Thimbleberry, Artists and Climate Change, Persimmon Tree, Headline Poetry and Press*, and *Terrain*. A chapbook of her work, *Poems in the Key of D Flat* was published by Overwrought Press, in 1992, and a collection of her poetry, *Jesus Christ Made Seattle Under Protest* was published by Finishing Line Press, in September 2019. She also has a poem appearing in *Support Ukraine* (anthology by Moonstone Press, 2022)

elainenussbaum.com
facebook.com/elainenussbaum.writer
Instagram: @ausernamethatisntalreadyused

About The Poetry Box®

The Poetry Box,® a boutique publishing company in Portland, Oregon, provides a platform for both established and emerging poets to share their words with the world through beautiful printed books and chapbooks.

Feel free to visit the online bookstore (thePoetryBox.com), where you'll find more titles including:

The Catalog of Small Contentments by Carolyn Martin

Earthwork by Kristin Berger

The Weight of Clouds by Cathy Cain

A Long, Wide Stretch of Calm by Melanie Green

Of the Forest by Linda Ferguson

Let's Hear It for the Horses by Tricia Knoll

Stronger Than the Current by Mark Thalman

Sophia & Mister Walter Whitman by Penelope Scambly Schott

A Nest in the Heart by Vivienne Popperl

Olympic by John Miller

Beneath the Gravel Weight of Stars by Mimi German

Tell Her Yes by Ann Farley

Late Fall Bucolics by Anne Coray

and more . . .

Printed in the USA
CPSIA information can be obtained
at www.ICGtesting.com
LVHW012335280524
781600LV00001B/151